BECOME A
RADIATION THERAPIST

by Kate Conley

BrightP◆int Press

San Diego, CA

BrightPoint Press

© 2021 BrightPoint Press
an imprint of ReferencePoint Press, Inc.
Printed in the United States

For more information, contact:
BrightPoint Press
PO Box 27779
San Diego, CA 92198
www.BrightPointPress.com

LIBRARY OF CONGRESS CATALOGING-IN-PUBLICATION DATA

Names: Conley, Kate A., 1977- author.
Title: Become a radiation therapist / Kate Conley.
Description: San Diego : ReferencePoint Press, [2021] | Series: Skilled and vocational trades | Includes bibliographical references and index. | Audience: Grades 10-12
Identifiers: LCCN 2020003762 (print) | LCCN 2020003763 (eBook) | ISBN 9781678200169 (hardcover) | ISBN 9781678200176 (eBook)
Subjects: LCSH: Radiotherapy--Juvenile literature. | Radiology--Juvenile literature.
Classification: LCC RM847 .C66 2021 (print) | LCC RM847 (eBook) | DDC 615.8/42 --dc23
LC record available at https://lccn.loc.gov/2020003762
LC eBook record available at https://lccn.loc.gov/2020003763

CONTENTS

AT A GLANCE

- Radiation therapists treat cancer patients. They provide radiation treatments.

- They work closely with doctors and nurses. Together, they create treatment plans.

- Approximately two-thirds of American cancer patients receive radiation therapy.

- Radiation therapists need a college degree. It can be a two-year or four-year degree. Most states also require them to be licensed or certified.

- Radiation therapists work with patients. They also use cutting-edge technology. This technology includes linear accelerators.

- Radiation can be dangerous. Radiation therapists must follow safety guidelines.

- Radiation therapist jobs are expected to increase in the United States. They may grow by 9 percent between 2018 and 2028.

- An aging population is creating the need for more radiation therapists. New advances in technology also provide opportunities.

WHY BECOME A RADIATION THERAPIST?

"**M**y sister was my motivation for choosing radiation therapy," says Erin Hendrickson.[1] She watched her sister battle childhood cancer. She admired the people who helped her sister. Hendrickson wanted to help too. So she became a radiation therapist.

Radiation therapists have important jobs that save patients' lives.

Hendrickson is one of 18,600 radiation therapists in the United States. She works with radiation every day. Radiation is a kind of energy. It travels through the air and is not visible. Radiation therapists use this

Radiation therapists are part of teams that treat cancer.

energy to treat diseases, such as cancer.

They operate powerful machines that emit

radiation. Most radiation treatments take

place in hospitals and clinics.

Radiation therapists choose the career for different reasons. Many want to help people. Radiation therapists work directly with patients every day. They form relationships with their patients during treatment. Radiation therapists also like being part of a health care team. It is rewarding to know that their work may save lives.

A student who wants to become a radiation therapist must undergo training. Students earn a degree in radiation therapy. They take classes such as **anatomy**. They also learn algebra and physics.

The elderly are at a greater risk of developing cancer. If they become ill, they may need radiation therapists to treat them.

They also learn computer science. During their training, they learn how to work with patients.

Radiation therapy is a growing field. People's risk of getting cancer increases as they age. The large aging population creates a higher demand for these therapists. New advances in radiation treatment are also emerging. Radiation therapy can be part of more patients' treatment plans. This also creates a higher demand. The positive job outlook makes radiation therapy a strong career choice. And the opportunity to help others makes it a rewarding one.

CHAPTER ONE

WHAT DOES A RADIATION THERAPIST DO?

Radiation therapists treat about two-thirds of all cancer patients in the United States. But radiation therapy is a relatively new job. It began in the 1950s thanks to a man named Henry Kaplan. Kaplan worked as a doctor at Stanford University. He was curious about a machine

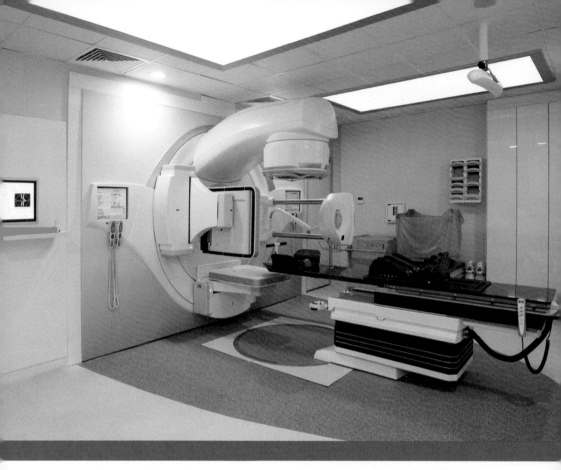

The linac is the machine most commonly used for radiation therapy.

he had seen. The machine was in the

physics department. It was called a linear

accelerator (linac).

Kaplan described the linac as

"miraculous."[2] It emitted X-ray beams.

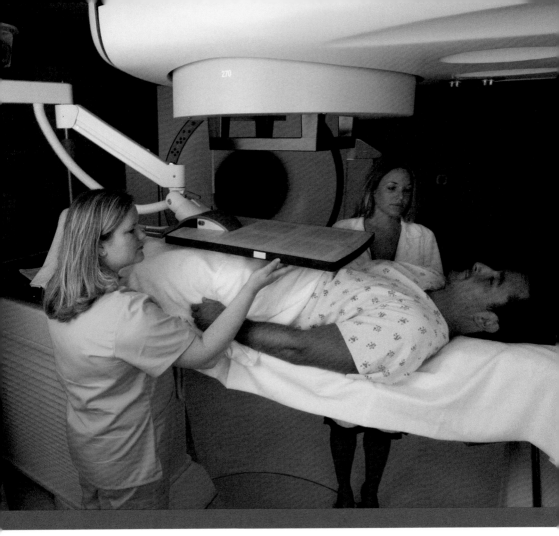

Radiation technology can help treat tumors.

They are waves of radiation. Their energy

is powerful enough to damage or kill

human cells. This includes cancer cells.

Cancer causes cells to grow out of control.

These cells form tumors. Tumors are abnormal growths of cells. These growths produce lumps in the body.

Doctors knew X-rays could kill cancer cells. But before the linac, this treatment was not always successful. The technology was not advanced enough yet. Most treatments provided only weak radiation. And it was hard for doctors to focus the radiation only at the tumor. This meant healthy **tissue** nearby was also damaged. Early X-ray treatments had other limits too. They could not reach tumors deep inside the body very well.

Kaplan hoped the linac might be the answer. It could target smaller areas. And its radiation was very powerful. Kaplan wondered if the beams could be used to treat cancer more effectively. It seemed like a promising idea. "I became convinced that this was to become the radiotherapy machine of the future," said Kaplan.[3]

TESTING IT OUT

Kaplan wanted to test his idea. He had a two-year-old cancer patient in mind. The boy had a tumor in his eye. In 1956, Kaplan treated the boy's tumor with the linac. The treatment worked. It removed the

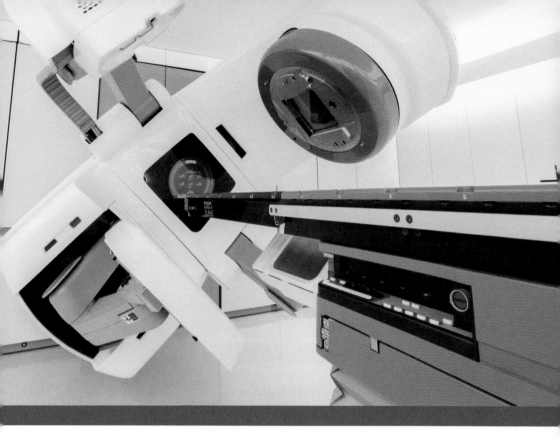

Radiation technology has advanced since Henry Kaplan's time.

cancer and saved the boy's eye. He was able to have normal vision. Kaplan's patient was the first to undergo radiation therapy using a linac.

The boy's successful treatment was a breakthrough. In the years that followed, scientists at Stanford improved the linac.

They made it more accurate. It could

target tumors very precisely. And it could

also make adjustments during treatment.

This was a key advance. Even if patients

EARLY RADIATION THERAPY

Wilhelm Conrad Röntgen was a German scientist. In 1895, he discovered X-rays. They allowed doctors to see inside a patient without surgery. This was the first time that doctors had been able to do this. They soon found additional benefits. In the early 1900s, doctors in France noticed the health of cancer patients improved when they were exposed to X-rays daily. Soon, X-rays became a new way to treat cancer. But the field was still new. It held many risks. The X-rays that cured cancer could also cause cancer later. Doctors at the time did not know this.

were perfectly still, parts of their bodies still moved. Their hearts beat. Their lungs moved as they breathed. And blood pulsed through their veins. Accounting for these small movements made radiation therapy safer and more effective.

More than 40 million people have been treated using a linac. Today's linacs can deliver radiation accurately. They can shrink tumors. They can also treat other symptoms caused by advanced cancer. These include pain or trouble breathing. In these cases, the radiation does not eliminate the cancer. But it makes the patient more comfortable.

WORKING WITH PATIENTS

Radiation therapists are at the center of these life-saving treatments. Most radiation therapists work in hospitals. They are part of a health care team. A doctor **prescribes** the treatment. Then the radiation therapist **administers** it to the patient. A typical treatment lasts fifteen minutes. Radiation therapists usually treat their patients five days a week. They do this for three to nine weeks.

Radiation therapists spend much of their time talking with patients. Before treatments begin, radiation therapists and

Radiation therapists develop strong relationships with their patients.

patients meet. The therapists explain what

to expect. Many patients may feel stressed

or fearful about their treatments. The

radiation therapist listens to their concerns.

They answer any questions. They help patients feel at ease and cared for during the treatments.

Building relationships with patients is important. "Every patient has a different story to tell and each one is meaningful," says Erin Hendrickson. "We . . . are with a patient every day . . . and relationships are formed in which you learn about them and their lives outside of their diagnosis."[4]

WORKING WITH TECHNOLOGY

Radiation therapists also work with cutting-edge technology. They are trained to use two machines. One is called a computed tomography (CT) scanner.

It maps the patient's body. The map is used

to find the tumor. The other machine is a

linac. It delivers radiation to the patient's

body. The radiation is usually in the form of

powerful X-rays.

OTHER FORMS OF RADIATION TREATMENT

Radiation treatment can take three forms. The first form is called external radiation. It is when a beam of radiation targets a tumor. The second form is called brachytherapy. For this therapy, doctors place objects that emit radiation directly into patients' bodies. The materials are removed after the treatment is done. The third form is called radioisotope therapy. In this therapy, a liquid that emits radiation is injected into the patient.

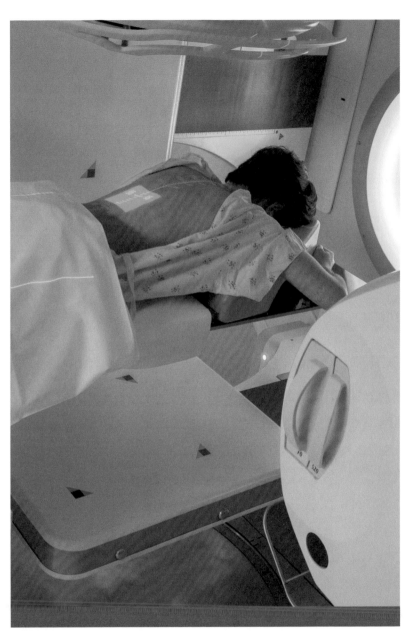

The X-rays from the linac are carefully targeted
so that the tumor site receives the most radiation.
The strong radiation can kill cancer cells.

During the treatment, the linac puts out radiation beams. It moves around a patient's body. Beams enter the body from several points. The point where the beams cross gets the strongest radiation. The goal is to cross the beams at the site of the tumor. Dr. Russ Altman is a professor at Stanford University. He interviewed Dr. Billy Loo, an oncologist. Oncologists treat cancer. The two talked about how the linac works. "You have a bunch of not-so-strong X-rays, but there's a lot of them coming into this point," explains Dr. Altman. "They add up so that the surrounding tissue gets a little bit. But that one point where it's all focused gets a lot."[5]

Radiation therapy is especially useful if a patient's cancer is caught early. Often, this means cancer cells have not spread to other parts of the body. In this case, radiation treatment alone may be enough to kill the cancer. Radiation therapy might still be used for cancer that has spread. But it is often combined with other treatments. Other treatments may include surgery or **chemotherapy**.

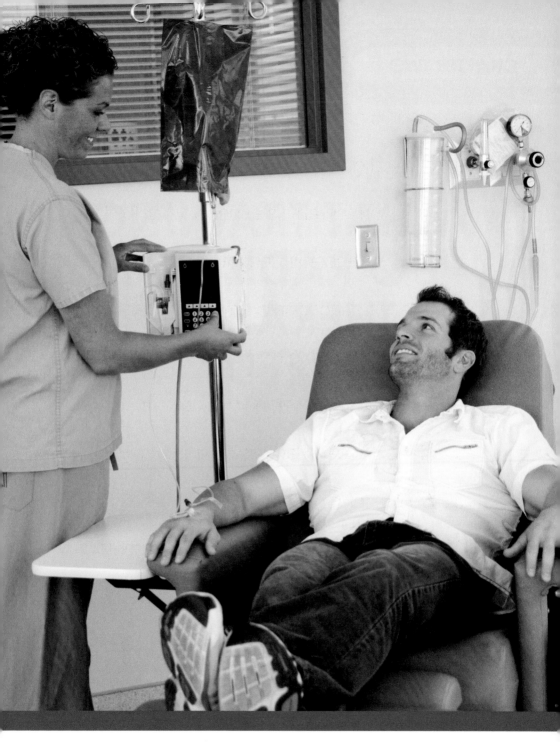

For some types of cancer, radiation and chemotherapy work better together than alone.

CHAPTER TWO

WHAT TRAINING DO RADIATION THERAPISTS NEED?

R adiation therapy is a challenging job. It requires therapists to be comfortable helping patients. Therapists must operate high-tech machines. They must also pay attention to details. "I believe it takes a really special person to

Radiation therapists work as part of teams with other medical professionals.

be a radiation therapist," says Heather

Mallett.[6] She directs the School of Radiation

Therapy. It is part of Northwestern Memorial

Hospital in Illinois. The program Mallett

leads is one of many. These programs

teach students the skills they need to

become radiation therapists.

Mallett believes the most successful students like working with people. She says, "The first thing I look at is character and personality. . . . People considering a career in radiation therapy need to be warm and compassionate. They need to be team-oriented and truly enjoy working with people." Mallet explains that "technical skills can be taught."[7] But it is difficult to shape a person's character and personality.

TWO PATHS

Radiation therapists can take two different paths to begin their training. One path is to earn a four-year degree in radiation therapy.

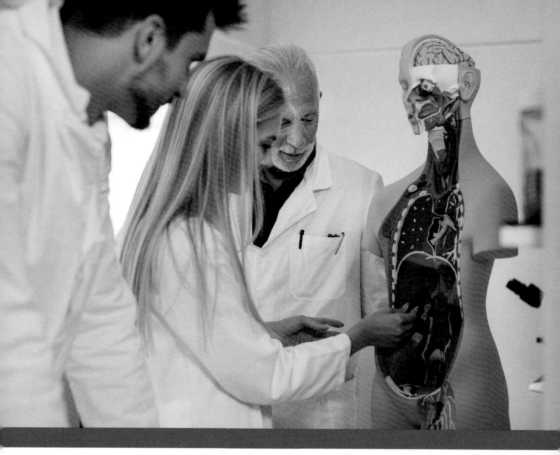

Health sciences training is required to become a radiation therapist. Therapists need a strong understanding of the human body.

This prepares students to begin work as

radiation therapists right after graduation.

Students take science courses. These

include physics and anatomy. They also

spend time doing clinical work. This means

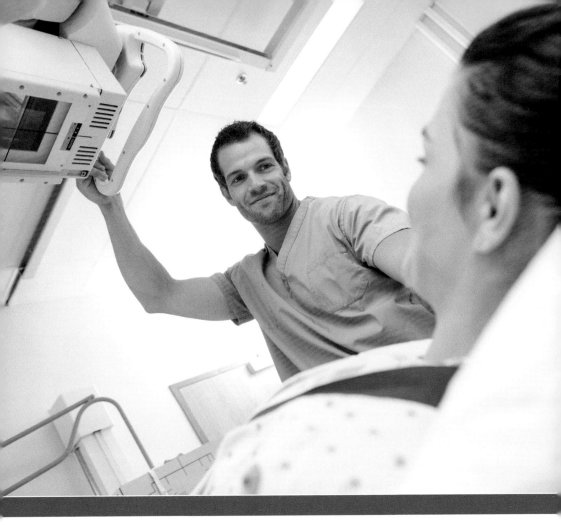

Radiologic techs operate X-ray machines.

they work directly with patients. They also

learn how to run the linac.

The other path is to earn a degree in

radiologic technology. The degree can

be two or four years. It prepares students to become radiologic techs. The students learn to use X-ray machines. They also train on CT scanners and other machines. These machines take images of inside patients' bodies. The images help doctors identify injuries and diseases.

Techs need extra training to become radiation therapists. They must attend a program on radiation therapy. It lasts one to two years. Students in the program spend about half their time in the classroom. They learn the science behind radiation therapy. They also learn to use the linacs.

They spend the other half of their time doing clinicals. Clinicals allow students to work directly with patients. Students also gain experience working on a team with doctors and nurses.

CLINICAL EXPERIENCE

Real-world experience is an important part of radiation therapy training. Working in a clinical setting provides this. Amanpreet Dhillon is a radiation therapist. She did clinicals as a student. "We get to use what we learned in class here," says Dhillon. "It's a little bit harder because technically, you aren't going to see a textbook-based patient. Every patient is different. Every disease is different. So it's a good challenge," she says.

Quoted in "Spend the Morning with a Radiation Therapy Student," YouTube, uploaded by Sunnybrook Hospital, November 4, 2014. www.youtube.com.

CERTIFICATION

Therapists may hold a license and be certified. They do this in addition to training. Some states require licenses. Licenses allow radiation therapists to work legally. Certification is different. Being certified shows that therapists have the necessary skills. They can do the job properly. It is an important step whether a student has a two-year degree or a four-year degree. Each state has different laws about certification. But most require radiation therapists to be certified. Most employers prefer certified therapists.

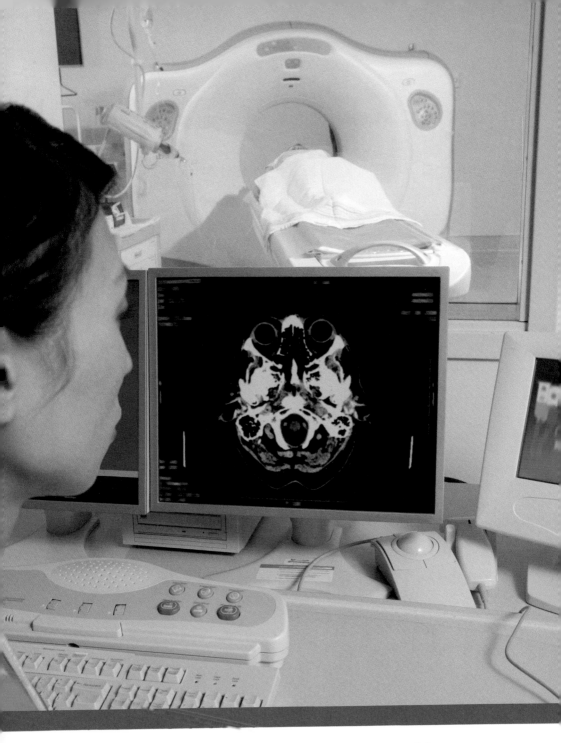

Certified radiation therapists can use machinery such as CT scanners on patients.

Therapists must pass an exam to become certified. It is given by the American Registry of Radiologic Technologists (ARRT). The exam tests a student's skills. It tests in several areas. They include using radiation safely, positioning patients properly, and providing quality care. Certified therapists must reregister each year. This keeps the certification up to date.

ADDITIONAL EDUCATION

Some radiation therapists choose to stay in that job for their whole careers. Others decide to go back to school. They often study subjects closely related to radiation therapy. One of those is medical dosimetry. Medical dosimetrists plan radiation treatments. They decide the best way to deliver **doses** of radiation. They base their plans on doctors' prescriptions.

Laura Brady made this career switch. She loved being a radiation therapist. But after eleven years, she wanted a new challenge. "I was ready to learn a new skill and grow professionally. So into dosimetry training I went," says Brady. "It is at times extremely challenging and most definitely

Radiation therapists must follow directions from doctors.

always rewarding. You are making a

difference in the life of a patient."[8]

Medical dosimetry programs are for people who have worked as radiation therapists. Each program is different. But most students must have at least three years of experience in the field. Students are also required to have a four-year degree. The degree can be in radiation therapy. Or it can be in a related field. Related fields include biology and physics. With this background, students can apply for a one-year program to become a medical dosimetrist.

In the program, students learn how to calculate a radiation dose. This requires

Radiation therapists can pursue additional schooling to become dosimetrists. They learn to calculate how much radiation a patient needs.

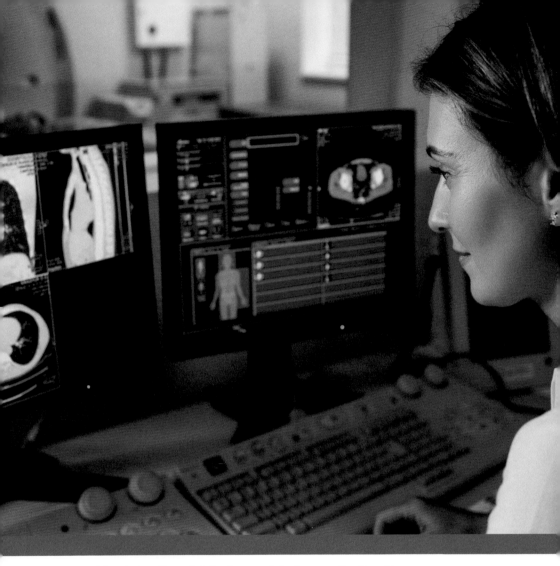

Most dosimetrists have higher salaries than radiation therapists.

great skill. The dose must be strong enough

to fight the cancer. But it cannot be so

strong that it kills healthy tissue. Students

who complete the program then take an exam. It is given by the Medical Dosimetrist Certification Board. Students who pass earn a certificate. Then they can begin working as medical dosimetrists.

OTHER CAREER OPTIONS

Some radiation therapists choose to stop working directly with patients. They use their skills in other ways. Some do medical sales. They work for companies that sell medical machines such as linacs. Others work for schools. They teach students how to become radiation therapists. Some radiation therapists also go into research or lab work.

CHAPTER THREE

WHAT IS LIFE LIKE AS A RADIATION THERAPIST?

Once trained, radiation therapists can begin working. More than 65 percent of American radiation therapists work in hospitals. They may also work in clinics or cancer treatment centers. In 2020, the median wage for radiation therapists was $84,367.

Most radiation therapists work a consistent, full-time schedule.

Most radiation therapists work full-time.

They normally work eight hours a

day. They work Mondays through Fridays.

Where Radiation Therapists Work

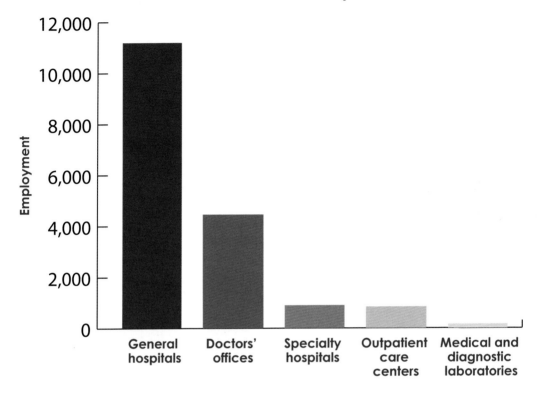

"Occupational Employment and Wages, May 2018: Radiation Therapists," Occupational Employment Statistics, US Bureau of Labor Statistics, *n.d. https://data.bls.gov.*

This schedule rarely changes. That is

because most treatments are scheduled

in advance. It is uncommon for a radiation

therapist to work weekends. Radiation

therapists rarely have to be **on call**.

ADMINISTERING TREATMENT

Radiation therapists begin each day

with safety checks. Their first task is to

examine the linac. This process is called

a quality assurance (QA) check. The QA

check makes sure the machine is working

correctly. Therapists make sure that it

moves properly. They check that it will

correct itself if a problem arises.

To begin the treatment, radiation

therapists enter data into the linac. The data

comes from a CT scan. They also enter

data about the dose of radiation. Then the

therapist positions the patient for treatment.

This is an important step. A patient must be

positioned correctly. If not done properly,

the radiation might not hit the correct part of

the body. This could damage healthy tissue

instead of the tumor.

LINEAR ACCELERATORS

Radiation therapists use linacs every day.
Linacs are huge machines. They measure
10 feet (3 m) tall and 15 feet (5 m) long. Patients
do not feel anything during treatment. But they
may hear a humming. Or they may notice a
slight smell from the electronics. Sometimes
they may also see beams of light coming from
the machine.

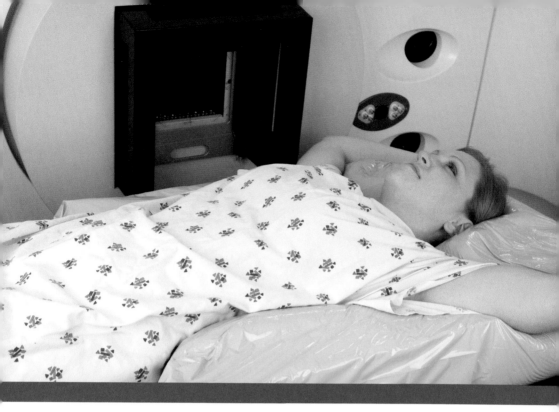

Radiation therapists may use molds to position patients properly and hold them still. This ensures the same area receives treatment every time.

Radiation therapists use equipment to position patients in the linac. They may use mesh masks or headrests. They may also use body molds. The equipment keeps the patient in the same position for treatment each time. Sometimes patients also have a dot tattooed on the radiation site. This is

a permanent mark. All these measures are

safeguards. They make sure the radiation

is delivered to the exact same place during

each treatment.

Therapists leave the room during the

therapy. This is another safety measure.

RADIATION MONITORING BADGES

Radiation can be dangerous. If radiation therapists are exposed to it every day, they face health risks. So they take many steps to stay safe. One is wearing radiation monitoring badges. These are small devices. Therapists clip these badges to their clothing. The badges record how much radiation the therapists are exposed to. This way they know if they have been exposed to too much.

Being exposed to radiation is dangerous. Therapists do not want to be exposed to it more than is needed. Instead, therapists observe patients on a monitor. Treatments can last from fifteen minutes to an hour. Patients and therapists can speak to each other through a speaker during a treatment.

When the treatment is over, a radiation therapist's work is not done. Therapists must record the treatment. The record includes the day's dose of radiation. It also notes any side effects a patient has had from the treatment. This could include symptoms such as headaches or soreness.

QUALITIES OF RADIATION THERAPISTS

Radiation therapists share many qualities. The biggest is a desire to help people. They enjoy working with patients. They feel rewarded assisting others. They like to help during a time of need. "I knew I wanted to be part of the treatment team that cared for and helped cure patients suffering from this terrible disease," says Kyle Garafolo. He is a radiation therapist. "I enjoyed the aspect of building a strong emotional bond with patients as they battle the disease."[9]

Most therapists are good with details. This skill is part of nearly every aspect of

Radiation therapists must be able to clearly communicate about a patient's health. It is important for the patient to understand how the treatment works.

the job. Therapists must notice even small changes in a patient's positioning. They monitor this from one treatment to the next. They must be sure the dosage in the linac matches the doctor's prescription exactly. And they notice any health changes in their patients.

Strong communication is another important quality. Radiation therapists often counsel their patients. They must clearly explain treatment plans and side effects. They also provide emotional support. They must be comfortable speaking to patients about problems or worries.

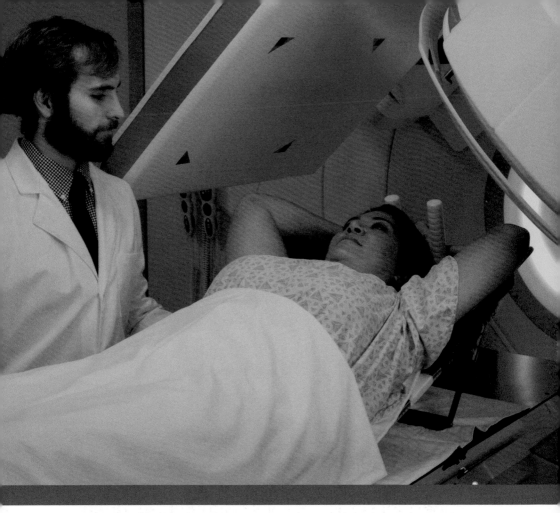

Being a radiation therapist requires physical and emotional strength.

Therapists must also communicate clearly

with doctors and nurses.

Additionally, most therapists enjoy

working with technology. The linacs they

Radiation therapists care deeply about their patients.

use are some of the most advanced

medical machines. Often, therapists are

also in good shape. This is important

because they stand for most of the day. They must also be strong enough to position patients.

JOYS AND CHALLENGES OF THE JOB

For most radiation therapists, helping others is the best part of the job. Many hospitals have a tradition for patients who complete treatment. These patients ring a bell. It is a signal that they beat cancer. Kirsten Wilcox is a radiation therapist. She explains the joy in that moment. "The coolest experience I had in this program was watching people finish treatment and 'ringing the bell,'" says Wilcox. "There is such a sense of

It is a tradition at many hospitals for cancer patients to ring a bell to celebrate finishing their treatment.

community and support that is hard to

explain. For the patient, it is a moment

of victory in the battle with cancer. It is

truly a joyous occasion in a very tight knit

community."[10]

Radiation therapists also face a difficult

side of the job. Despite best efforts,

radiation therapy cannot save every patient.

This is one of the hardest parts of the job.

Therapists see patients daily for weeks.

They talk, share stories, and become

friends. But not all cancer cases can be

cured with radiation. Therapists know

they are doing their best to help patients.

But sometimes even their best work cannot save patients' lives.

This is a bittersweet feeling for many therapists. Garafolo talks about this challenge. During his work, Garafolo has treated many patients. He has helped babies to elderly adults. "I've developed countless relationships with many of my patients that I will forever remember and cherish," says Garafolo. "Unfortunately, this fight is a journey that is not always won."[11]

Radiation therapists must be mentally strong when their patients do not get the results they hoped for.

CHAPTER FOUR

WHAT IS THE FUTURE FOR RADIATION THERAPISTS?

Radiation therapists' future looks good. The US Bureau of Labor Statistics (BLS) projects job growth. It estimates a 9 percent increase in radiation therapist jobs. This increase would happen between 2018 and 2028. That is about 1,600

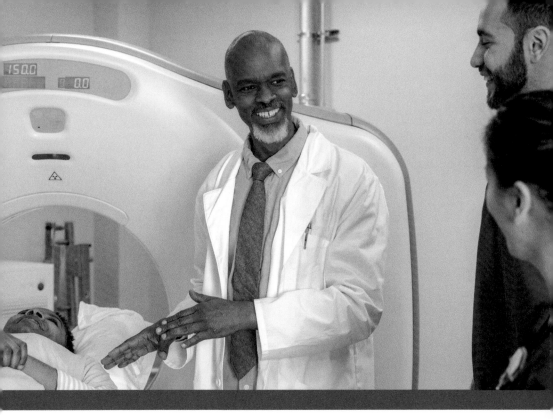

There is a growing need for radiation therapists.

new jobs. This growth is higher than the

nation's average job growth. That average is

estimated to be 5 percent.

AN AGING POPULATION

An aging population is part of the reason

for this growth. People's risk for cancer

increases as they age. Sixty percent of new cancer cases occur in people age sixty-five and older. In 2000, 35 million Americans were sixty-five and older. This number will double by 2050. The number of cancer cases will likely grow too.

Radiation therapy can be a good option for aging patients. Older cancer patients

A RISE IN HEALTH CARE JOBS

The BLS looked at the years 2018 to 2028. Eighteen of the top thirty fastest-growing jobs during that decade will be health care jobs. Radiation therapy is one of these jobs. The jobs also include personal care aides. Nurse practitioners are listed too. Most of this growth is due to the aging population.

have special needs. Many patients already have other health problems. This can make treating cancer more difficult. They may not be strong enough for treatments such as surgery or chemotherapy. Radiation therapy is less **invasive**. Aging patients can often handle this treatment more easily.

NEW TECHNOLOGY

New technology is also helping radiation therapy grow. Scientists are working on a new way to deliver the therapy. It is called PHASER. PHASER gives radiation in a flash of light. The current treatment takes minutes to an hour. A flash lasts less than a second.

Since the flash is shorter, the radiation used in it must be much stronger.

PHASER is an important development. It eliminates problems caused when patients move even slightly. Patients may make tiny movements, such as breathing. This can affect the placement of the radiation. Flash technology avoids this problem. The flash means a patient has to remain still for only a moment.

Dr. Billy Loo is an expert in radiation therapy. He sees promise in PHASER. It makes the treatment more precise than ever before. Dr. Loo explains that more

PHASER technology is similar to a camera flash.

precision can kill cancer without causing

additional damage.

Cancer researchers can use mice as test subjects. Experiments with mice help predict whether new equipment and drugs are safe for humans.

In 2020, this treatment was still being tested. But the results are positive. It was tested on mice. The flash radiation worked as well as or better than regular radiation. And it was much less likely to damage healthy tissue. This suggests the human body would react similarly. The body may respond better to a high-dose flash of radiation than to a longer, lower dose of radiation.

Scientists are making other advances in radiation therapy. One is a drug known as IPdR. The drug weakens cancer cells. Then the patient undergoes radiation therapy. The drug makes the radiation more successful. The radiation destroys the cancer cells better since they are already weak. The drug also causes few side effects in patients.

REACHING OUT TO STUDENTS

Medical advances are expanding the field. As a result, the demand for radiation therapists is growing too. Organizations are reaching out to students. These organizations are in the field of radiology.

INCREASING ACCESS

Radiation therapy is a powerful cancer treatment. But it requires large, expensive machines. They can only be operated safely by trained therapists. These factors limit many countries' access to radiation therapy. Scientists are trying to change this. They are working on smaller and safer machines to deliver radiation. The machines would also be less expensive. These advancements could save thousands of lives in the future.

They want to attract more therapists.

The American Society of Radiologic

Technologists (ASRT) has created an

outreach program. It is called Radcademy.

Radcademy is a website for teenagers.

It has short articles and videos. They show

what careers in medical imaging are like.

Radcademy informs on a variety of topics.

It talks about X-ray machines and radiation

therapy. It introduces a technical field in a

fun, engaging way.

Dr. Sal Martino is proud of radiologic

technologists. He wants to share this

pride with a new generation. Martino is an

ASRT leader. He explains that radiation therapists use life-saving technology every day. Martino says, "It's crucial that we educate the public about the important work radiologic technologists perform."[12] Radcademy aims to help achieve that goal.

Programs like Radcademy make radiation therapy better known. Radiation therapists have been using this technology to save lives for more than fifty years. During those years, radiation therapy has improved. It has become safer, faster, and more precise. Today, radiation therapy is one of the most powerful weapons in the fight against cancer.

The goal of programs like Radcademy is to encourage teenagers to become radiation therapists.

administers

provides something, such as a treatment

anatomy

a branch of science about the structure of the human body

chemotherapy

a type of cancer treatment that uses powerful chemicals

doses

specific amounts of medication, radiation, or other forms of treatment for patients

invasive

involving putting surgical instruments or other objects into a person's body

on call

away from work but available to work if needed

prescribes

writes instructions that allow a patient to receive a type of medicine or treatment

radiologic

related to the science of X-rays or other forms of radiation

tissue

a group of similar cells that form parts of a body

SOURCE NOTES

INTRODUCTION: WHY BECOME A RADIATION THERAPIST?

1. Quoted in "Why I Chose to Become a Radiation Therapist," *OncoLink*, March 27, 2013. www.oncolink.org.

CHAPTER ONE: WHAT DOES A RADIATION THERAPIST DO?

2. Quoted in Mitzi Baker, "Medical Linear Accelerator Celebrates 50 Years," *Stanford Report*, April 18, 2007. https://news.stanford.edu.

3. Quoted in Baker, "Medical Linear Accelerator Celebrates 50 Years."

4. Quoted in "Why I Chose to Become a Radiation Therapist."

5. "Billy Loo: 'Flash' Radiation Therapy," *The Future of Everything,* March 5, 2019. https://engineering.stanford.edu.

CHAPTER TWO: WHAT TRAINING DO RADIATION THERAPISTS NEED?

6. Quoted in Erinn Hutkin, "Radiation Therapists," *Chicago Tribune*, October 26, 2014. www.chicagotribune.com.

7. Quoted in Hutkin, "Radiation Therapists."

8. Quoted in "Why and How Did I Become a Dosimetrist?" *OncoLink*, March 13, 2013. www.oncolink.org.

CHAPTER THREE: WHAT IS LIFE LIKE AS A RADIATION THERAPIST?

9. Quoted in Hutkin, "Radiation Therapists."

10. Quoted in "Radiation Therapy Program (Minnesota)," *Mayo Clinic College of Medicine and Science*, n.d. https://college.mayo.edu.

11. Quoted in Hutkin, "Radiation Therapists."

CHAPTER FOUR: WHAT IS THE FUTURE FOR RADIATION THERAPISTS?

12. "Radcademy Inspires Young Learners," *ASRT News Room*, January 29, 2016. www.asrt.org.

FOR FURTHER RESEARCH

BOOKS

Emma Huddleston, *Work in the Health Care Industry*. San Diego, CA: ReferencePoint Press, 2020.

Kevin Kurtz, *The Future of Medicine*. Minneapolis, MN: Lerner, 2021.

Barbara Sheen, *Great Jobs in Health Care*. San Diego, CA: ReferencePoint Press, 2019.

INTERNET SOURCES

"Radiation Therapist," *Explore Health Care Careers* (blog), *Mayo Clinic College of Medicine and Science*, n.d. https://college.mayo.edu.

"Radiation Therapists," *Occupational Outlook Handbook, US Bureau of Labor Statistics*, September 4, 2019. www.bls.gov.

"Radiation Therapy," *TeensHealth*, January 2019. https://teenshealth.org.

WEBSITES

The American Registry of Radiologic Technologists (ARRT)
www.arrt.org

The ARRT is a leading organization for radiology professionals in the United States. It provides certification and registration for people who work in all branches of radiology.

American Society for Radiation Oncology (ASTRO)
www.astro.org

ASTRO is the world's leading organization for radiation professionals. Its members are health care professionals who work in radiation therapy. They treat more than 1 million cancer patients each year. The society provides training, sets standards, and advances research.

Radcademy
www.asrt.org/radcademy

The American Society of Radiologic Technologists created Radcademy. This website teaches young people about radiation therapy and medical imaging technology.

ABOUT THE AUTHOR

Kate Conley has been writing nonfiction books for children for more than a decade. When she's not writing, Conley spends her time reading, drawing, and solving crossword puzzles. She lives in Minnesota with her husband and two children.